Paul Manning's first book, *How to be a Wally*, gave offense
to literally millions. His name is now a household word
along with Domestos, Broba

D0545550

also by Paul Manning and published by Futura

HOW TO BE A WALLY
1984 AND ALL THAT

SUPER WALLY!

The *advanced* Wally manual

PAUL MANNING

A Moon and Parrot Publication
from

Futura

A Futura Book

First published in 1984
by Futura Publications, a Division of
Macdonald & Co (Publishers) Ltd
London & Sydney

ISBN 0 7088 2604 0

Photoset in North Wales by
Derek Doyle & Associates, Mold, Clwyd
Printed in Great Britain by
Hazell Watson & Viney Limited,
Member of the BPCC Group, Aylesbury, Bucks

Futura Publications
A Division of
Macdonald & Co (Publishers) Ltd
Maxwell House
74 Worship Street
London EC2A 2EN

A BPCC plc Company

CONTENTS

INTRODUCTION

Wallies – they're all around us. From the Watford Gap Service Area, where they've taken the tops off the litterbins, put them on their heads and are now running around the car park pretending to be Daleks, to the Palace of Westminster, where they're busily trying to reduce the entire country to a state of complete Wallydom as quickly and expensively as possible – everywhere you look, the cult of the Wally has the nation in its grip.

Hardly surprising, then, that the question is being asked more and more frequently: what is a *Super*wally, and how do I become one?

The plain answer is that if learning how to be a Wally requires hours, days, weeks and even months of practice, then becoming a Superwally can take a lifetime – and even then, many still fail to make the grade.

Princess Anne, for example, seemed set fair to become one of the great Superwallettes of recent times – constantly swearing at journalists, pouting sulkily at photographers, falling off her horse at equestrian events ... But then, just as she seemed in line for a permanent place in the Superwally Hall of Fame, off she went, travelling round the Third World on behalf of the Save The Children Fund and making rather gamey jokes about lorry-drivers on the Australian Parkinson Show – hardly the behaviour of a potential Superwallette.

On the other hand, Mark Phillips has the distinct look of a major Superwally of the future. Not only does he make a habit of plunging head first into the waterjump at Badminton every year, but on those rare occasions when he actually manages to string a few words together, he invariably says the wrong thing – and with an effortless brilliance that immediately puts him yards ahead of the nearest competition.

But the dividing-line between success and failure in the Superwally stakes is perilously thin. To illustrate *how* thin, one need only point to the case of Tony Blackburn. Last year, he was looking like the ultimate Superwally DJ: Superwally jokes, Superwally false laugh, a regular Superwally show on Superwally Radio London. But then, one grim night in Kensington, he blew it all by responding with quiet and completely uncharacteristic dignity when a group of Ra-Ra Wallies led by Princess Di's Superwally brother tried to take his trousers down in a restaurant. Tony came up against bigger Superwallies than himself and found himself in what David Coleman would describe as All Sorts of Trouble. Result? Years of painstaking effort down the drain.

Then there was Neil Kinnock, who seemed a cert for Superwallydom when he fell flat on his back in the sea while posing for the cameras on his day of triumph in the Labour leadership contest. He was shaping up nicely – until he did something that no serious contender for Superwallydom would ever do: he tried to laugh it off and make a *joke* of it all.

So what does it take to become a Superwally?

Easy to sum up, but horribly difficult to achieve.

Superwallydom means being a Wally, and then some. It means, for example, staying up until three in the morning and phoning up K-tel simply to see if they really *do* operate a 24-hour ordering service. Or moving lock, stock and barrel to Crystal Palace in the hope of getting a better picture on your telly. It means queuing for days and then getting trampled underfoot in the stampede for Cabbage Patch Dolls in the January sales. Or wearing a hunting-knife strapped to your calf and genuine ex-Vietnam

GI combat jacket plastered with skull and crossbones and SAS insignia, then fainting at the sight of blood.

In other words, it means doing all the things a Wally would do, but then, just when everyone thinks you couldn't be more of a Wally if you tried, crowning it all by doing something so crass, so breathtakingly stupid it leaves your audience gasping with admiration.

For example, we all knew that Mark Thatcher was a Wally. But it wasn't until he got lost in the Sahara and brought half the Moroccan air force out looking for him that we realized he was a Superwally too.

We all knew that Fay Hiller, Dick Emery's frilly-knicker sex siren, was almost certainly a Wallette; but when she appeared at the comedian's funeral and posed for the cameras in a skin-tight leatherette suit with plunging neckline and thigh-length bootees, she immediately rocketed into the Big League as one of the great Superwallettes of the year.

We had all heard that President Chernenko was a bit of an old Wally, but it was only when he paused in the middle of his five-hour inaugural address as Soviet leader to allow the batteries in his pacemaker to recharge that we knew that he, like his opposite number in the White House, was a Superwally too.

Or take Hughie Green – obviously a Wally. But when he tried to film *Opportunity Knocks* on board a nuclear submarine to show his support for the government's defence policy, got the sack, then went around bleating that the Governors of the BBC and IBA were all part of the same gang and that they phoned each other up to say, 'Screw Hughie Green,' he exceeded the expectations of even his stoutest fans.

Likewise Prince Andrew. We all had him down as a Wally long ago; but when he sprayed white paint all over the international Press corps, then pretended his finger had slipped, he proved beyond any doubt that even in the face of some stiff competition from the rest of the family, he was far and away the biggest royal Superwally of them all.

And of course, we all had our suspicions that John Selwyn Gummer was a Wally, but it wasn't until recently that we saw how seriously we'd underestimated his talents. For when he revealed that he has the words SEX SEX SEX and YES YES YES emblazoned on his pillows and followed that by insisting that the Press drop the 'Selwyn' from his name, everybody did just that – and he's been John 'Superwally' Gummer ever since.

Can anybody become a Superwally?

By now it should be clear that there are some people in this world who start off with a significant advantage in the Superwally stakes. If, for example, you fall into one of the following categories, you should stand a better than average chance of successfully Going For The Big One:

- A member of the cast of *Coronation Street*
- An ex-mistress of a recently deceased comedian
- A football manager whose only scores are with other people's wives
- A brother or near-relation of Princess Di
- A team member on *A Question of Sport* (especially if you wear a diamond-patterned cardigan and engage in sickening banter with David Coleman)
- A sex-symbol from *Dallas* or *Dynasty*
- A guest on *The Price Is Right*
- An expatriate small-time villain living with a tubby peroxide blonde in Marbella
- One of the Nolan Sisters

If you're not included in the above list, don't give up. By carefully studying this book you will gain comfort, inspiration and encouragement as you tread the long, lonely road ahead. But do bear in mind that Superwallydom can't be achieved overnight. Whether you choose to Go For The Big One by crossing the Atlantic in a bathtub, or pushing a supermarket trolley up Ben Nevis, remember: you *won't* be a Superwally if you succeed on the first attempt.

The Superwally Promise

Superwally! is a fully comprehensive guide which covers every aspect of the subject, from 'Little Wally's First Words' to 'The Art of Wally Seduction', on past 'Occupational Therapy for the Elderly Wally' to 'What to do with a Dead Wally's Ashes'.

And to show that the author and publishers of this book have complete confidence in its effectiveness in every case, we are prepared to offer a unique and unprecedented guarantee.

If any Wally, having bought a copy of *Superwally!* and read it thoroughly from beginning to end, genuinely believes that he has not become a Superwally as a result, then he has the right to return to the shop where he bought it and say, 'I have bought this copy of *Superwally!* and I can honestly say I'm as sick as a parrot, because frankly it just hasn't worked for me.'

The bookseller will then fall about laughing, and when he recovers, grasp him by the hand and say:

'Congratulations, son – you've made it at last!'

INTRODUCING THE WALLETTE

There was a time, not so long ago, when any argument about equality between the sexes came down to the same old question: 'All right, then, if women are equal to men, how come there's not been one major female Wally in the whole of history?'

No one has ever been able to come up with a satisfactory answer. Some have put it down to lack of opportunity, others to a conspiracy on the part of male Wallies down the ages. Then again there were those who said that if Sir Arthur Bryant had been born female, our island story would have been given an entirely different slant.

But whatever the excuses, the fact remains: the way of the Wally has always been as truly masculine as the Great Smell of Brut.

Yet now, thanks to huge advances in social awareness, the daily efforts of countless Starbirds and Sun Page Three girls and, above all, the untiring leadership of such national figures as Pamela Stephenson, Erika Roe and Joan Collins, the serious business of being a complete and utter Wally is no longer exclusively a male preserve.

This is the age of the Wallette.

A Superwally should be able to spot the average Wallette immediately as she totters over the horizon on her platform heels, clutching her Snoopy bag and wearing her Duran Duran tee-shirt, but for mere Wallies who have not reached that level, here are her vital statistics:

Language

The Wallette's favourite words and phrases are 'out of order', 'winkle', 'the fellers', and 'You gotta laugh, eh?'

- Sitting around with other Wallettes in playgrounds, chewing bubblegum with her mouth open, talking about boys and swearing at children who ask her if please can she get off the swings now so they can have a go.
- Hanging around day after day outside the Radio One office in the vain hope of catching a glimpse of Peter Powell.
- Going to the disco and swaying around on the dance floor with another Wallette, staring into space, wishing a feller would come along and telling him to bog off when he does.
- Failing her driving test three times on the trot, even though she was showing most of her thighs the last time.
- Crying over a Mills and Boon romance at the launderette.
- Always carrying a toothbrush and a spare pair of knickers in her handbag just in case.
- Getting tiddly on port and lemon and then going on to a club to watch a male stripper, hooting with laughter and screaming, 'What d'you call that?' at the climax of his act.
- Going to Ann Summers coffee mornings and buying crotchless panties that she'll never dare wear.

Professions

Favoured Wallette professions include receptionist, barmaid, secretary, stripogram artiste, holiday tour guide topless waitress and prime minister. But without doubt the most popular career is that of Office Wallette.

The Office Wallette is usually from a temp agency, and has photographs of Lewis Collins, Nick Heyward and Prince William stuck over her desk beside a sign that says DON'T BLAME ME – I ONLY WORK HERE! Next to the typewriter lie:

1) A copy of *Honey* opened at the astrology page
2) An ashtray with a half-smoked, lipstick-stained Players No. 6 in it
3) A year's supply of nail varnish and false eyelashes
4) An *Over 21* address book filled with the phone numbers of endless other Wallettes

The Wallette will spend most of the day making phone calls to her Wallette friends, saying things like 'Then *he* said –' or 'I thought, cheeky sod, I thought –' or 'No, I couldn't, not just like that, not there, could I, no, well anyway I did –' or 'I could have *died*, honest, I've seen bigger matchsticks, I just didn't know where to look.'

Occasionally a Wally in the office makes the mistake of asking the Office Wallette out for a date. The next morning, she comes into the office smirking gruesomely at the other girls and crooking her little finger significantly.

Every year at the office party, the Office Wallette gets drunk and insults the managing director. A bit later she traps him in the car park and apologizes to him in floods of tears. As he backs away, seeking the safety of his Ford Granada, she launches herself at him with a French kiss, fails to make contact and hits the deck heavily as he speeds away. Later she invites the office junior to take her home and he's too frightened to say no. But once they get home, she passes out before anything can happen. The next morning her mind's a complete blank and she can't remember a thing about the previous evening.

Just as the Wally spends most of his time Getting One Down, saving up for some Go-Faster stripes for his Escort and watching the wrestling on Saturday afternoon with the curtains drawn, surrounded by empty cans of Black Label and half-eaten packets of Monster Munch, the Wallette spends most of her time either thinking about, preparing for, or recovering from a night with 'the fellers'.

Although she is extremely active in this area, none of her relationships seem to last very long. This is because:

1) She is a Wallette
2) She goes out with Wallies
3) A change is as good as a rest, innit?

What sustains the Wallette through the hurly-burly of her less than satisfactory love-life is the fantasy that one night she'll be down at the Moon and Parrot with the girls after work, when she spots, sitting by himself in the corner, a face that seems strangely familiar to her. At that moment he glances up at her, almost shyly – and her heart misses a beat. Now she knows who he is. Those flashing green eyes. Those chiselled features. Those dark, flowing locks. It's what's-his-name from the smash ITV series for all the family *Robin of Sherwood*. He seems anxious to get away from the Moon and Parrot – after all, at any moment he could be recognized by one of his millions of fans. Muttering that she has to go and powder her nose she walks towards the door marked 'Hens'. As she does so, their eyes meet, as if to acknowledge the fierce, almost animal attraction for one another that they are both already feeling. Without a word he stands up. They walk out of the pub together. For a moment his hand softly touches her forearm as he opens the door of his gleaming white Lamborghini. She steps inside, settling back into the deep bucket seats, which smell intoxicatingly of real, expensive leather. There's the hint of a mischievous twinkle in Robin's green eyes as he smoothly eases the low-slung sports car into gear. 'Shall we

... go?' he whispers. And with a surge of power, pressing her deeper into her seat, Robin is soon whisking her away to his luxurious £150,000 Surrey mansion, where she will no longer just be a Wallette, but the mystery blonde who, my spies tell me, is now the live-in girlfriend and constant companion of TV's newest superstar ...

In fact, the Wallette is not over-fussy about who finally rescues her from the leering Wallies at the Moon and Parrot, so long as he's famous and sexy. But she'd prefer it if he was one of the following:

1) Robin of Sherwood
2) Lewis Collins
3) Prince Andrew
4) Indiana Jones
5) The blond Wally in Wham
6) Jeremy Irons
7) Sting
8) Boy George
9) Peter Powell
10) Simon Le Bon

Superwallettes

The sad fact is that, unlike Wallies, Wallettes rarely have the staying power, the sheer dogged determination that it takes to Go For The Big One. Most reach a certain stage in their life when the fight goes out of them, they stop giggling and talking about winkles and become relatively normal.

On the other hand, there are a few Wallettes who are shining exceptions to the rule: Wallettes who have not only gone on to become Superwallettes, but who have actually built a career on their superb qualities in this area. Contrary to what many people think, this is not merely a question of appearing in front of the cameras as often as possible. Anna Ford clearly thought that was the case, but somehow has always failed to be a convincing Superwallette. Her Majesty the Queen, in spite of temptations that most of us would be unable to resist, has failed dismally in this regard. *We are not a Wallette* ...

Sarah Kennedy, too, was In All Sorts of Trouble when she moved from the Superwally show *Game For a Laugh* to *Sixty Minutes*, which was merely boring. In fact, it was beginning to look as if Sarah would never make the grade. But then she Went For The Big One, first by revealing that she was looking for someone to father a little Kennedy baby and then publicly changing her mind about the whole thing on television the following night — a sequence of events which won her the Order of the Sick Parrot in perpetuity.

Barbara Cartland and Barbara Woodhouse are natural Wallettes.* Joan Collins was almost certainly born a Wallette and finds it all as easy and natural as stripping off for *Playboy* at the age of fifty.

Then there's Pamela Stephenson, who should one day write a book about her heroic attempts to achieve Superwallettehood. At first, she appeared to have no chance when starring in *Not The Nine O'Clock News*. Then she started taking her top off in fashionable London restaurants and hiding under the table — classic Wallette behaviour. Unfortunately she suffered a major setback when she had a baby by Billy Connolly, who's nothing like a Wally. But now that she's once again appearing on the front of the *Daily Star* in a see-through blouse and silly dark glasses, it's beginning to look as if she's made it at last.

---

* Being called Barbara is undoubtedly an advantage if you want to be a Superwallette, as Barbaras Cartland, Woodhouse, Windsor, Bach (Ringo's Wallette) and Edwards prove. Interestingly, the name Ken, Kenny or Kenneth (as in Barlow, Everett, Lynch, Dalgliesh, Newman of the Yard and Robinson) confers a similar advantage on Wallies.

THE WALLY SUTRA

Throughout his life, every Wally finds himself a prey to all sorts of odd urges and strange, irresistible compulsions. The urge, for instance to press the little WAIT button on Pelican crossings, even when he hasn't the slightest intention of crossing the road; or to summon lifts in office blocks or department stores just for the hell of it; or, when at the cinema, to stand up just beneath the projectionist's box and entertain the rest of the audience by casting silhouettes of swans, ducks, flapping eagles or perhaps just his own thick head on the screen below. Nobody knows why he does these things – least of all him.

But without doubt the strangest and most baffling of all his compulsions is the mysterious desire that overcomes him once in a while to try and get off with a member of the opposite sex – even when bitter experience has taught him that this is the quickest known route to a slap in the face or a knee in the goolies, and that any successful docking-manoeuvre with a Wallette can be relied on to introduce all manner of hideous and unwanted complications into his life.

Since he's aware of the appalling pitfalls involved, the more circumspect Wally therefore does his best to ignore his troublesome sexual urges for as long as possible, and instead limits himself to the following tried and tested Wally sex substitutes:

1) He sidles up behind a likely-looking Wallette as she pores over a copy of *Oh Boy!* at the local John Menzies, pinches her bum, then either runs like hell or retires nimbly to a safe distance and pretends to be engrossed in the latest issue of *The Railway Modeller*.
2) He whistles at girls from the driving seat of his Capri, so that at the first sign of danger he can pull out from the

kerb and hare off down the road with a merry laugh and a squeal of tyres.

3) He leers down the barmaid's cleavage as she pulls him a pint, then goes 'GOORRRRR' with appropriate Wally body language while she rolls her eyes heavenwards and slouches off to serve another customer.

4) He plasters his motor with suggestive window stickers, e.g.:

- IF YOU FEEL SEXY, SMILE
- MAKE LOVE NOT WAR – SEE DRIVER FOR DETAILS
- FLASH YOUR LIGHTS IF YOU HAD IT LAST NIGHT
- SEX INSTRUCTOR – FIRST LESSON FREE

5) He moons out of coach windows at passing cars.

But eventually, of course, valuable as they are, these various forms of Wally para-sexual activity are no longer enough for him. The sinister stirrings from the region of his patterned nylon jockey briefs can no longer be denied. No matter how he fights it, sooner or later every Wally feels a need for the Real Thing.

In other words, he needs to Get A Bit.

Getting a Bit

If you've ever listened to a group of Wallies bragging about their sexual exploits as they hammer the Space Invader machine at the Moon and Parrot or dust themselves with great billowing clouds of Brut talcum powder in the locker room at the local sports centre, you might be forgiven for thinking that, as a would-be Wally Superstud, you're going to have to spend twenty-four hours of every day on the job. Nothing could be further from the truth. A quick fumble on the back seat of the motor every now and then is ample for most purposes – and, suitably embellished, it'll furnish you with raw material for quite enough outstanding tales of your superhuman sexual prowess to keep you going for at least three months, which, incidentally, is roughly how long it'll be before you start feeling your oats again.

Of course, that makes the whole business of Getting A Bit sound ridiculously simple – and it isn't. In fact, as any experienced Wally will know, it's considerably more complicated than it first appears – particularly in the uncut version of *Do You Come Here Often?*

So here to help you through those tricky early stages is a step-by-step guide to the art of Wally seduction, with real-life examples of the kind of problems you may encounter at each stage.

Step 1 What to wear when you're on the pull

First of all, when you're out combing the pubs and discos for the Wallette of your dreams, it pays to be correctly dressed. There's no accounting for taste, especially among Wallettes, and for some reason, the combination of a sweat-stained 'I'm With Stupid' T-shirt and a pair of sagging Levis that expose a half-moon of pink, spotty buttock every time you squat down to retrieve a dropped No. 6 coupon just isn't generally regarded as much of a turn-on.

No. You need Wally dress sense.

There are certain accoutrements that will mark you out immediately as a Wally of distinction. A St Christopher medallion is essential, obviously; so is a tight-fitting tailored shirt undone to the naval. And when it comes to the hardware, a good general rule is to load your fingers and wrists with as many chains, identity bracelets, Korean-made signet rings and Des O'Connor-style personalized diamanté cuff-links as you can manage without having to walk around with a permanent stoop – unless of course you're a happily married Wally looking for A Bit On The Side, in which case it's wise to leave the identity bracelet at home.

So you're now in full Wally combat gear, and you're hot to trot. A splash of the Great Smell of Brut behind each ear and half a pint down the jockey briefs for good measure and you're ready to go. But first, let's deal with a couple of common grooming problems.

'My problem is, I'm one very hairy guy – I mean, REALLY hairy! Last time I took a girl on a date, she accidentally brushed against me with a lighted cigarette and the whole of my chest went up in flames. I'm very worried about it as the lads at work all call me Godzilla and I'm afraid it could affect my chances with the girls.'

'Ape Man' of Balham

The rest of us should be that lucky. If there's one thing that's guaranteed to bring the Wallettes flocking, it's the sight of a broad, manly torso crowned with a luxuriant crop of bushy chest hair. Take no notice of your mates, they're just jealous – but maybe next time keep a pocket fire extinguisher handy for emergencies.

'I daren't go out on the pull because of this giant spot on my chin. I've tried everything but it just won't go away. Is there anything I can do? It's really making my life a misery.'

'Pimple' of Enfield

Short of having it surgically removed or burnt off with a blowtorch, the answer is No. But don't stay home moping about it – get out and find a Wallette with the same problem. That way you can spend hours discussing all the lotions, potions and patent remedies you've tried and you'll establish a valuable common bond for when the time comes to get down to cases.

Step 2 Finding a Wallette and making your move

Finding the kind of spot where Wallettes hang out isn't hard: every town has its cattle-market tucked away somewhere. It's getting a Wallette on her own that's the problem. Wherever you go, whether it's down at the pub or on the floor of the disco, you'll find that for some reason every available-looking female has a girlfriend in tow who looks at best like a member of the Russian Olympic weight-lifting squad and at worst like an extra from a Fellini movie – and sometimes the two of them are so inseparable you begin to wonder if you're going to have to pour coconut oil all over them and prise them apart with a crowbar.

If the five most beautiful words in the English language are 'Buy one, get one free', the six most deadly have *got* to be 'Mind if my friend comes too?' So make sure you have a game-plan for precisely this situation: a range of stylish opening gambits designed to sweep the Wallette of your choice right off her feet and force her to ditch Number Two at the earliest opportunity. For example:

'Hey, where have you been all my life?'
'Hey, has anyone ever told you you look just like the dark one in Bananarama?'
'Hey hey hey, you're a big girl. Ever thought of doing a centrefold for my mates at *Penthouse*?'
'Pinch me – I think I'm dreaming!'

The rest is plain sailing – or it should be ...

'I keep on seeing this amazing girl down at the local disco and I really fancy her something rotten. I'm sure I've seen her somewhere before: maybe in a magazine, or on TV – maybe even in a past life ...?

'I long to pluck up courage to talk to her, but I can tell she's not like all the other girls and I'm afraid of making a fool of myself. What should I do?'

'Lovesick' of *Luton*

You should get one thing straight for a start: unless you're a top-class Superwally like Prince Andrew, Mark Thatcher or Oliver Reed, you're never going to Get A Bit with models, debs or TV personalities. If God had meant you to score with the Anna Fords and Selina Scotts of this world, he'd have given you a receding chin, a private income and a fleet of brand-new BMWs.

You're a Wally. Your only chance of success is with a Wallette. It's tough, but that's life.

> *'I've never had any problem chatting up the girls. My trouble is, whenever one of them reaches past me for her handbag or brushes against me on the floor I get so excited I have an accident in my Y-fronts. Is this what's known as premature ejaculation and if so, is there a cure?'*
>
> *'Hair-trigger' of Harlow*

Sadly, this is a common problem and there's not much you can do about it except to try and concentrate on something else until the danger's passed. Try thinking about something really boring to take your mind off it. The SDP's chances in the next election, the Public Sector Borrowing Requirement, Bobby Robson's use of the 4-2-4 formation in the Big One against Luxembourg, or, if all else fails, try remembering the name of your Euro-MP.

Step 3 The Crunch

Once you've managed to extricate your chosen Wallette from the melée of gyrating bodies and you've screamed a few endearments into her ear above the blare of the jukebox or PA, you're then faced with a tricky decision. Where's it to be? Round the back for a quick one, and face the usual 11.15 bottleneck? The back seat of the motor, and risk attracting the attention of other Wallies, who'll leer through the window, hammer on the roof and put you off your stoke by going 'Waauurrrr!' or yelling other forms of ribald encouragement from the pavement outside? Or back to your place, where you'll be expected to engage her in time-wasting conversation about star signs, the boss's BO, what Boy George said to Wogan on telly the other night, and apologise for the embarrassing beer and TV dinner stains on the sheets?

Let's assume it's the latter. And now comes the really difficult part: the actual act of Getting A Bit.

One of the major causes of sexual maladjustment among Wally couples these days is the assumption on the part of the Wally that every Wallette is up and ready and raring to go as quickly as he is. On the contrary: she needs a fair bit of coaxing, wheedling and general tuning up before she's in the mood.

So instead of launching yourself at her with a cry of GERONIMO-O-O-O!!! the moment you get inside the front door, show a bit of consideration: pause, count to ten, and ply her with a piece of traditional Wally foreplay, e.g.:

'Right – get 'em off then.'

Then switch off the lights, clamber on top of her and let Nature take its course.

'I thought my luck was in the other night when I saw this gorgeous bird winking at me from over the other side of the room at this party at my mate Wally's. But when I took her back to my place for a quick bonk, she got into a right state and started going on about how she was fed up with being treated as a sex object and how men were only interested in one thing and wouldn't it be nice if once in a while instead of trying to prove how bloody virile they were they'd just sit you down in the kitchen like any normal human being and have a cup of tea and a chat.

'What I want to know is: Where did I go wrong?'
'Puzzled' of Peasedown

Human sexual relations are a complex thing, and in the course of that infinitely subtle, infinitely suggestive interplay that makes up the Wally mating ritual, it's all too easy to misread the signs – especially when you've staggered round every pub and disco in town in search of a bit of spare and you're so pissed you can hardly stand up. So, be warned; don't mistake a 'Hands off' for a 'Come hither'. It's very tempting to believe that the girl making eyes at you across the dance floor is panting for a night of steamy passion, when in fact all she's doing is trying to dislodge a piece of grit from her contact lens.

> *'When it comes to sex, I've always reckoned I was as broadminded as the next man, but the other night I don't mind telling you I got the shock of my life. I was just getting down to basics with this bit of fluff I'd picked up outside the chippie, when all of a sudden she stops and says, "Hang about. I know a different way. Why don't we try it with me on top." I showed her the door right sharpish, I can tell you! But then later I started wondering: I mean, it did sound a bit ... well, you know, kinky – but so what? Supposing she had a point there? Did I do the right thing?'*
>
> *'Strangeways' of Streatham*

The answer to this is that as every Wally knows, there's really only one Wally love position: it's called the One Over The Eight, and it involves the Wallette lying flat on her back with one eye on the clock in case she misses the last bus and the other on the letters page in *Honey*, while you're spreadeagled on top of her, desperately trying to husband your energies so that you don't pass out in a drunken stupor in mid-performance.

But on the other hand, if being a Wally stud means anything at all, it means notches on bedposts – and whether you choose to Get A Bit standing up, lying down or swinging from a chandelier, a score is still a score.

Step 4 The Follow-Through

It's commonly supposed by most newcomers to the art of Wally seduction that by this stage you're home and dry: that all that remains is to scrub the lipstick off your collar, take a quick shower followed by another thorough dousing with the Great Smell of Brut to disguise any lingering whiffs of Body Mist, 4711 or poncy Menthol cigarettes, then hurry back down to the pub or wherever to give the lads an in-depth blow-by-blow post-match commentary.

If only life were that simple. In fact, in nine cases out of ten what happens is that instead of basking in the afterglow, you now have to weather a storm of tears and recriminations as the Wallette launches into either:

'You won't tell my Dad will you promise you won't tell my Dad he'd bloody kill me if he found out'

or:

'Am I on the pill what do you mean am I on the pill that's bloody typical of a man that is of course I'm not on the pill what kind of a girl do you take me for'

or:

'You bloody men you're all the same you're only interested in one thing I suppose it's never occurred to you a girl has feeling oh no a quick leg-over that's all you're after and anything in a split-seam skirt and platform heels is fair game well I'll tell you something big boy we're not all brainless dollybirds you know we're not all like that fat tart Lesley oh yes I saw you giving her the eye so don't you come the little innocent with me we're not all silly bits of fluff you can pick up and chuck away when the fancy takes you and there is such a thing as respect you know course I don't suppose you'd know the meaning of the word and you needn't think just because a girl lets you touch her up in the carpark it means she wants to leap into oi I'm talking to you and you can put away that dirty mag too if you don't mind you know something your type really make me want to throw up you and your tight trousers and your mirror shades and your hullo darlings and your gold bloody chains and your Ford bloody Cortinas you really fancy yourself don't you you really reckon you're a stud well let me tell you something I've had more fun staring at a crack in the wall you're all bloody mouth that's your trouble course I blame myself I mean I should have

*known I don't know why I bloody fall for it it's the same
every time I must need my bloody head examined ...'*

It all underlines the central timeless paradox at the heart
of the Wally mating game, namely that only a complete and
utter Wally would ever attempt to Get A Bit with a
Wallette. On the other hand, only a Wallette would let him.
   You just can't win.

WALLY FAMILY LIFE

At a certain age – say in his mid-to-late twenties – the average Wally begins to feel that there's more to life than motors, Carling Black Label and *The Price is Right*. He wonders whether at his age he ought not to be looking for something more lasting, more meaningful and life-enhancing than simply pushing other Wallies around the shopping-precinct carpark in supermarket trollies every Saturday afternoon. He may even ask himself whether the time has come for him to think of someone other than himself, of his long-term future and prospects.

At this point, more often than not, he'll pull himself together, say 'On yer bike, my son – time to Get One Down you' and adjourn swiftly to the Moon and Parrot, where a bunch of other Wallies, who like as not have also just experienced the same painful microsecond of introspection and self-doubt, are already Going For It and are on their second pint. And usually that's the end of that.

But then sometimes, as he listens to Wally from down the road telling his one Little and Large joke for the third time that night, as he laughs dutifully and says, 'Like it, like it,' with all the other lads, he suffers another twinge of unease.

What could be wrong? The lads are there. They've all got enough down them now to have a rowdy game of darts and sing along with *Sailing* on the jukebox, leer at a few Wallettes, then go out to the car park and throw the litter bins about. So why this strange feeling that there should be more to life than this?

The answer is that being a complete and utter Wally all the time simply isn't enough for him any more. He secretly hankers after intimate evenings watching *Terry and June* on the Sonyvision, cuddled up in front of the safe and economical Living Flame natural gas fire. He dreams of building utility sheds in the back garden with shiny Black and Decker tools, now and then biting into a Mars Bar, while his own little Wallette watches him fondly from the kitchen window, where she's doing the washing up again. He pictures himself trudging up the garden path with a sunny smile and muddy boots and asking, 'What's for lunch, love?' while she shakes her head, ruefully eyeing the great clods of earth he's just brought into the house and says brightly, 'Birds Eye Cod Fillets, of course,' and he smiles again and starts tucking in while she contentedly mops up the muddy floor ...

In other words, he wants a home, a wife and, above all, the chance to make lots of Little Wallies.

And just to make sure there are no problems in the Little Wally department, the average Wally usually gets his Wallette in the club well before the topic of marriage is broached. This has the added advantage of making it look as if his rampant need to Get A Bit at all costs has caused him to be forced into marriage by family and other pressures. Because of course, no serious Wally should ever admit to his mates that he actually *wants* to settle down and raise a family.

Settling Down

Just because the Wally now has a better half, there's absolutely no reason why his basic lifestyle should change significantly in any way whatsoever. It's possible that for a few months he won't feel the need to go 'Gooorr!' whenever a Wallette walks by, but after a while, even this habit will return and life will go on much as before.

Until, that is, the arrival of Little Wally.

Bringing up Little Wally

Some people are born Wallies (one thinks immediately of
Jeremy Beadle, Cyril Smith and Jonathan King), some
achieve Wallydom (Torvill and Dean, John Selwyn
Gummer), and some have Wallydom thrust upon them
(anyone selected to represent Great Britain in the
Eurovision Song Contest). But unless you're utterly
convinced that you've produced a born Wally (and these
are still relatively rare), then it's wise to give Little Wally
every chance in life by bringing him up to be at least as big a
Wally as you are, and if possible a bigger and better one
too. Fail to make that effort and literally anything could
happen: a scholarship to Oxford at the age of twelve, good
works among the starving millions of the Third World, a
brilliant career with the Royal Shakespeare Company, or
worse.

Remember – you can't start too early.

The first months

In these early months, it's simply a matter of peering into
his cot when you come back from the Moon and Parrot and
making as many quintessentially Wally faces or noises as
you can manage without giving yourself more of a headache
than you have already. Child psychologists have confirmed
that the sight of a huge, friendly face with unfocussed,
bloodshot eyes and crisp crumbs around the mouth, and the
familiar smell of Watney's Red Barrel as it wafts over the
cot can have a formative influence on the very young.

But bear in mind that even Little Wally has a brain,
however miniscule. So gradually move from making
friendly Wally noises – 'Goooorrr!', 'We-haay!', 'Oroight?'
and 'Whaaaat?' – to actual words and phrases. There can

be no greater thrill in family life than hearing Little Wally mouth his first words. If you have been relating to him in the correct way, they should be one of the following:

'Like it'
'Magic'
'Nice One'
'Tasty, tasty'
'On yer bike'
'Come on you Spurs'
'Wallee' (pointing at you)
'Yer jooookin'

The early years

It is absolutely vital that Little Wally learns to express himself, develops his own character, discovers his own strengths and weaknesses, fights his own fights and becomes an individual Wally in his own right as early as possible. At the same time, it's also absolutely vital that he avoids doing any of this while you're trying to watch *Crossroads*, cracking open a few cans of lager with the lads while the wife's out shopping, having a meal or doing the pools.

So Little Wally will need a sense of discipline – some basic rules to live by:

1) Whenever he makes any kind of noise or tries to speak, say 'Shut up, you!' and ignore him. Many of the best brought up Little Wallies can reach the age of six or seven still believing that their name is Shutupyou.

2) When the lads come round for a drink, don't make him feel left out: give him a can of Black Label too. At first, he'll just mess around with the ring top – the tricks he learns now will serve him in good stead at the office party in a few years' time – but after a while he'll start imitating you: Getting One Down, smacking his lips noisily and lisping, 'It's what your right arm's for'.

3) Encourage him to make his presence felt at the local play group by knocking over other children's piles of

bricks, asking the Little Wallettes if he can see their bottoms, leaving a Farley's rusk soaked in milk on the play-leader's chair and nutting the other little Wallies for no particular reason. Once in a while you may find he's been nutted back by one of them, in which case you should pay a visit to the Daddy of the Little Wally responsible and threaten to push his teeth so far down his throat he'll have to stick a toothbrush up his bottom to clean them.

4) Always make him climb the highest slides in the playground. If he succeeds, it'll show he's got bottle – as important a quality for a little Wally as for a big one. If he doesn't and falls flat on his head from a great height, don't worry: it'll probably improve his chances of growing up to be a complete and utter Wally no end.

5) Never encourage him to mix with little girls who may already have discovered that one of their missions in life is to cramp the style of Wallies, be they little or big. On the other hand, if he insists on inviting some little Wallettes round for tea now and then, don't panic, but refer to his prowess down at the pub later, e.g.:

'Gor, you should see my Little Wally – he can't half pull the birds! Had three of them round at our place today. Going to be a right little tearaway, he is.'

'Chip off the old block, eh?'

'This is it.'

Some early signs of Wallydom in the young

Every Wally father remembers that proud moment when, through some particularly ignorant or moronic word or deed, his son proves that he's got what it takes to Go For The Big One. All your efforts were worthwhile: Little Wally's going to Get It Right.

There are endless tell-tale signs for the watchful parent. For example:

- He falls asleep face-down in a bowl of Milupa.
- He swallows his dummy.
- He treads on a Carling Black Label can and clunks up and down the street with it bent around his foot.
- He ties all the swings together in the playground so that it takes the park attendant half an hour to untangle them.
- He writes WALLY 4 TRACY on the bus shelter when he doesn't even know a Tracy.
- He goes round to other little Wallies' houses while their parents are away to watch the latest video nasties.
- He does wheelies on his BMX bike and falls flat on his back.
- He charges into a game of football being played by kids at least five years younger than him and scores ten goals, doing a John Motsom imitation at the top of his voice.
- He cuts out *Sun* Page Three girls and keeps them in his bottom drawer but doesn't really know why.
- He starts collecting highly toxic novelty rubbers in the shape of biscuits and liquorice allsorts and offering them round to all his friends.
- He wins £5 and a Reporter's Certificate by getting a letter published in the 'What's Your View?' column in the *Junior TV Times*. E.g.:

'I used to enjoy Game For a Laugh I thought it was brilliant, it was all comedy and fun, I wish it was back on telly. Matthew Kelly was great and so was Jeremy Beadle as well. Fraggle Rock is good too it is so enjoyable and interesting that even our dog Biff sits down and watches it. Everyone can fall in love with the cute little doozers except my dad of course he is usually asleep then.'

'Fragglefan' (10) Humberside.

Toys

The most important thing about Little Wally's toys is that you should be able to enjoy playing with them when he's at school or asleep. There's not much fun to be had from a Baby Bouncer or Postman Pat video, but you can get hours of enjoyment from riding around on a baby's first tricycle.

Other toys worth investing in are:
- A climbing frame which collapses under your weight
- A Steve Davis mini-snooker set
- An Eric Bristow Junior Dartboard
- A Colonel 'H' Action Man
- A BMX bike
- A large-scale Build-Your-Own Cruise Missile set, complete with transport vehicle.

Little Wallettes

There's no getting away from it: even in this day and age it's considerably more difficult to bring up real little Wallettes than real little Wallies. So, when the Wally father discovers that the tiny creature he's been dandling on his knee for the past two years is a girl, not a boy, he'll probably mutter something about it being a Bit of a Choker When All's Said And Done and take no further interest. Until, of course, she starts going out with a boyfriend, when he'll look up from the television and say something to the effect of: 'If that idle layabout gets you into trouble, you're out on your ear, girl – I kid you not.'

However, for the Wally who prefers to play a more active part in bringing up a right little Wallette, there are two basic rules to remember:

1) Get her a bra and makeup set as soon as she's out of nappies.
2) Put her down for an audition with *Minipops* before her fifth birthday.

WALLY'S BEST FRIEND

There's absolutely nothing wrong in wanting to keep a pet if you're a Wally. But remember – many an instant character appraisal has been formed on the basis of what pet you own, so Get It Right. No one will take you seriously as a Wally if, for example, you wander around a shopping precinct with a peregrine falcon on your shoulder and a couple of pedigree pointers trailing along behind you.

Choosing a pet that will enhance your status among other Wallies is a tricky business, but here are some basic guidelines:

Pets a Wally can be seen with
An Alsatian
A Doberman Pinscher
A greyhound or whippet
An English Mastiff
Any large, stupid-looking mongrel
A ferret
A parrot that says 'Nice one, Cyril'
A goldfish for Little Wally

Pets a Wally should never be seen with
A thoroughbred racehorse
A polo pony
A golden eagle
A golden retriever
Any kind of big cat
Any kind of domestic cat
A labrador
A rabbit
A gerbil

Some Wallies have made a bold bid for originality by keeping pairs of miniature poodles, naming them Dot and Carrie or Benson and Hedges, and dressing them up in neat little tartan coats for when the weather turns chilly. On the whole, though, it's advisable to play safe and go for a large, ugly, potentially dangerous brute that's guaranteed to put the fear of God into postmen and Old Age Pensioners and leave nice big turds in people's front gardens.

Naming your Wally Pet

This is relatively straightforward. All Wally pets should of course be male – in fact, they should as unmistakably and impressively male as possible – so the range of names you have to choose from is somewhat limited.

Avoid anything amusing, fancy or clever. Go for something with true Wally style, plus a hint of thoroughly masculine menace, e.g.:

  Biff
  Starsky
  Clint
  Gnasher
  Rex
  Tebbit
  Gummer

Training your dog the Wally way

Don't bother about training the brute when he's inside the house, apart from administering the odd kick whenever he's in range and beating him soundly if he farts during mealtimes. And don't overfeed him either – that rangy, ribby look as he tugs ferociously on his choke-chain will earn you impressed looks from the other Wallies on your street. Training your dog the Wally way involves:

1) Brutalising and humiliating him by lengthy and pointless sessions in the park: you on one side, yelling

'*Stay, Biff*!' at the top of your voice; Biff rummaging around in a litter bin three hundred yards away, taking not a blind bit of notice.

2) Encouraging him to mate energetically with anything in sight – cushions, chair legs, lamp-posts, Jehovah's Witnesses, Avon ladies, etc.

3) Allowing him to let off steam by rushing up to small children, snarling and baring his teeth. As the child is led away in hysterics, laugh and tell the parent he's just being friendly.

4) Dressing him up in a bow tie and a paper hat, sitting him on a piano stool, filming his performance on video and sending it off to *That's Life*.

THE WALLY AND THE IVY

There can be few more magical moments in the Wally family calendar than the arrival at long last of the season of Black Carling, Good Beer and random Breath Tests: Yuletide.

Everything is prepared. The decorations have been up since the beginning of November. The little silver Christmas tree is laden with those candles, baubles and fairies that weren't smashed to pieces during last year's New Year's Eve party. There's a MERRY XMAS sign on the front door just under the plastic Santa which you bought from Woolworths four years ago and which now looks more like Frankenstein's monster. There's a keg of bitter in the corner and some sparkling wine in the fridge for the day itself. The wife's parents have settled into the usual pre-Christmas torpor and are already complaining about the way Little Wally exposes himself out of the front window to passers-by. The hangover from the office Christmas party is now little more than a distant buzzing in the ears and there have been no embarrassing phone calls, so presumably that little episode in which you gave the Wallette from accounts your number after checking out her bottom line down behind the photocopier must have been a figment of your imagination.

Mrs Wally is already a bit giggly because she's been Getting It Down Her in the kitchen with the cooking sherry, which was meant for the trifle. Little Wally is Over The Moon because he's sure he's going to get a BMX bike at last.

You're primed and ready for the perfect Wally Christmas.

Some really magic Christmas presents, together with the thoughts that count

From Mum to Dad:

A power tool kit. ('Hope he drills a hole through his bloody foot.')

From Dad to Mum:

A Marks and Spencers Summer Gift Voucher. ('I warned her I didn't have much time to buy presents, didn't I?')

From Dad to Little Wally:

A model Dinky Toy BMX bike. ('Didn't say how big it was going to be, did I?')

From Mum to Little Wally:

A Radio One 'Hullo Mate' badge. ('Thank you, Peter Powell.')

From all the Wallies to Granpa:

A Starbird Calendar. ('That should keep him happy, the randy old so-and-so.')

*From all the Wallies to
Granma*:

Winifred Atwell's Christmas
Party. ('Serves her right for
giving it to *us* last year.')

*From Granma and Granpa
to Dad*:

Six cans of alcohol-free
lager. ('Not that he'll take the
hint, the Wally.')

*From Granma and Granpa
to Mum*:

A Baby's First Words
Album. ('Well, it's not right
Little Wally being all on his
own like that.')

*From Granma and Granpa
to Little Wally*:

A BMX bike. ('That'll show
the poor little beggar what
tight parents he's got.')

- Guess how far into *The Sound of Music* Granma will fall asleep and start snoring.
- Guess which is going to come first: 'The Hills are Alive With The Sound Of Music' or Granma waking up with a start when her false teeth fall out.
- Think up an original excuse for leaving the family and nipping down to the Moon and Parrot where all the other Wallies will be singing 'The Twelve Days of Christmas'.
- See how many items of furniture you can smash while trying out Little Wally's BMX in the sitting room.
- Try to find the duff bulb on the Christmas tree lights in under two hours.
- Guess what Mrs Wally got mixed up with the brandy that makes the Christmas pudding taste so odd.
- Guess who'll be the first to say *either* 'I remember when Christmas used to be a real family occasion' *or* 'It's not the same without Eric and Ernie' *or* 'Next year we're going to spend Christmas in a hotel in Margate and have done'.
- Guess when, and on whom, Little Wally will bring up the entire box of Milk Tray he's been scoffing on the quiet.

- 'I don't know why you lot don't go to church like we did when we were young – it *is* His bloody birthday today in case you hadn't noticed.'
- 'If certain members of this family who shall remain nameless had lifted a *finger* to help in the kitchen instead of sitting around getting drunk, you'd have *got* Christmas dinner before four o'clock.'
- 'It *is* a turkey – it just shrunk a bit in the oven.'
- 'No, that's just way out of order, Granpa. I do not invite you to spend Christmas in my home just to have you stinking the place out after the Christmas pudding.'
- 'We know you want to watch *Where Eagles Dare* but Mummy wants to watch *The Sound of Music* and Christmas is Mummy's day, isn't it?'
- 'I don't care if Daddy does want to watch *Where Eagles Dare* – he's done sod all to help today so you can all bog off down to the park for a couple of hours 'cos I'm watching bloody Julie Andrews so there.'
- 'I hate Christmas I hate Julie Andrews I hate turkey I hate you all and I'm going to smash you all with my BMX bike and then I'm going to smash my BMX bike too.'
- 'He's not a spoilt little brat and if you and Granma don't like it here you can bog off back to the home for all I care and don't bother to come back next Christmas, you geriatric old git.'
- 'Don't you abuse my father like that, you ignorant Wally, or I'll tell everyone about a certain call I had yesterday from a certain someone in Accounts who had a certain experience down behind the photo-copier at a certain office Christmas party, you randy old sod.'
- 'I still say there was no need to throw the remains of the turkey all over the carol singers.'

THE COMPUTER WALLY

Not even the most uninformed Wally can fail to have noticed that this country is currently in the grip of a major technological revolution. New industries are sprouting up, old ones are going to the wall. Everywhere you look, it's micro-this or micro-that. Even in the shops, the comforting jingle of the old-fashioned cash register is being replaced by the electronic chirrupings of the latest computerised check-out till. Like it or like it not, it looks as if the Mighty Micro is here to stay.

So it seems reasonable to pose the question: what impact is all this having on the Wally in the street?

Well, as far as the vast mass of ordinary run-of-the-mill Wallies are concerned, the answer is: depressingly little. Along with ninety per cent of the rest of the population, most Wallies are unashamed Luddites who only come into contact with the New Technology once a year when they spill half a gallon of Black Label over the firm's computer at the office party. And of course you only have to mention the words Silicon Chip for one of them to chime in with the obligatory joke about this Irish geezer who went into this shop and asked for one so they gave him one in a bag and he said hang about where's the salt and vinegar geddit ber-boom HURR-HURR-HURRR. It's a sad fact that probably the first time the computer boom impinged on the consciousness of the average Wally was when the manager at the local W.H. Smith's rearranged the magazine racks to make room for all those glossy computer journals – the result being that *Auto-Car, Bike, Men Only* and *New Directions* were banished to the top shelves and Joe Wally found himself having to stand on a step ladder to read them.

But among a small, perhaps more forward-looking section of the Wally population, things were rather different. Never slow to jump on a bandwagon, this advanced breed of Techno-Wallies soon realized that, properly used, the computer brought with it a golden opportunity to waste more time more pointlessly and cause bigger and better administrative cock-ups than at any previous point in human history. They perceived the simple truth: that just as every home, office or small business would one day have its own computer, so each home, office or small business would one day have its very own resident *Computer Wally*.

How to become a Computer Wally

Before the advent of the home computer, Computer Wallies were a rare and élite breed to be found only in the bosoms of large corporations and the accounts departments of the nationalized industries. And so, for many years, the incomparable thrill of accidentally wiping off the entire divisional sales figures for the past three years, playing frisbee with a collection of floppy discs, or adding a couple of extra noughts to an Old Age Pensioner's gas bill was only vouchsafed to a privileged few.

But thanks to the recent boom in small, inexpensive home computers and the fact that Dragons, Nords, Spectrums and the like are now falling off the backs of lorries up and down the country, Computer Wallydom has at last come within the reach of all – and at a cost roughly equivalent to no more than a few nights' serious drinking down at the Moon and Parrot.

Step 1 Buying your Home Computer

This is not nearly as difficult as it sounds – so chuck away all those computer mags and 'Which Computer' colour supplement pull-out guides for a start. Basically it all boils down to a question of *either*

a) Going for a dirt-cheap TI-99 and then finding there's no software to go with it. *Or*

b) Splashing out a whole week's beer money on one of the really pricey models and then finding that if there *is* any software to go with it, you can't afford it.

Step 2 Teething troubles

By the time you've installed your Wallytron 2000, spent hours trying to figure out how to program it, taken out your frustration on the wife, kids, Alsatian and anybody else within range, and finally given up on it and stormed off to the Moon and Parrot with a splitting headache, leaving the computer to the tender mercies of Little Wally (who, needless to say, mastered it weeks ago with effortless aplomb), you may well be tempted to ask yourself why you bothered to buy the bloody thing in the first place.

And you won't be the only one, either. Your mates will probably be asking you the same question. Don't be thrown by this: even the most accomplished Computer Wally occasionally comes in for a bit of good-natured ribbing from the lads. Simply silence them with one of the following carefully prepared and totally specious stock answers:

Rough Translation

I mean, after all, basically it's the computer age, innit?	*Next door's got one.*
I mean, I didn't want Little Wally to miss out, did I?	*I thought it'd keep Little Wally off the streets.*
I mean, you've got to think of the kid's future, haven't you?	*Honest, I had to do something – it was that or Borstal.*
'Course, it's not a toy.	*'Course, to him it's just a toy.*
It's *educational*.	*I don't know why I bothered.*

He's learning these amazing things off it.	*All the little bastard does all day is sit in front of it, crash-landing Jumbo Jets.*
Taken to it, like a duck to water, he has.	*I just can't get him off the bleeding thing.*
He's even using one at school now.	*It's the same at school.*
That's what it's all about really – it's, like, training him to take his place in the society of the future.	*It's a bloody waste of the taxpayers' money, if you ask me. At this rate the only qualification that kid's going to end up with is a CSE in bloody Space Invaders.*
'Course, I'm getting to grips with it meself now.	*'Course, I'd use it meself only I haven't got two brain cells to rub together.*
It's ever so useful in the home.	*You can do the Pools on it, you know.*
And the beauty of it is, *all the family can get involved.*	*Trouble is, what with Little Wally and his Jumbo Jets and Granpa hooked on VIOLENT UNIVERSE, I can't get a bloody look in.*
See, it's user-friendly – even a child of four can work it.	*Stone me, even the wife's had a go.*

Step 3 Getting the Best out of your Wallytron 2000
Having overcome the early difficulties, every Computer Wally now experiences a momentary pang of guilt: here, sitting on his breakfast bar, is a highly sophisticated piece of electronic hardware – and so far he's failed to use it for anything more demanding or intellectually stimulating than the odd game of PSST!, Pac-Man or Asteroids. So after many, many painful hours dinning into his skull the rudiments of computer programming, he now finds he has to wrack his brain to think of some potentially more

worthwhile use to which to put it.

Mercifully, this stage is short-lived, but to carry you over it, here are a few ideas:

- Logging the Alsatian's feeding times.
- Running a private computer-dating scheme.
- Providing up-to-the-minute details of the current state of your account with Take Six, Harry Fenton, MFI and Augustus Barnett.
- Plotting the wife's biorhythmic cycle.
- Calculating the mother-in-law's life expectancy.
- Attempting to access top-secret Ministry of Defence data-banks for details of the latest cruise missile deployments, then trying to flog the story to the *Guardian*.
- Keeping a computerized record of the previous season's racing results, so you can tell at the press of a button whether it's worth risking a fiver on Golden Boy at 15 to 1 in the 2.30 at Newmarket.

But of course, a computer is only as good as the information you feed into it. And after you've spent an entire evening tapping on to the computer a list of all the people you plan to send Christmas cards to, only to find that when you call up the results on the screen they're totally unintelligible because you were half pissed at the time and got all the addresses muddled up, you may well find that disenchantment begins to set in again. At which point it's high time to cut your losses and resign yourself to the fact that basically you're going to end up using your computer just the same way as every other Computer Wally from Land's End to John O'Groats. In other words, you're going to play games on it.

Step 4 A Brief Guide to some Wally Computer Games
Given the vast range of mind-bogglingly tedious Computer Games on the market, you should have no difficulty here. Simply select two or three of the more spectacularly Wally ones and you'll soon find yourself becoming so hooked on them that you're as dependent for survival on your hourly dose of JET SET WILLY as a junkie screaming for his fix.

In fact, it won't be long before all normal family life goes by the board, those carefree nights puking your guts up in the car park of the Moon and Parrot are nothing but a distant memory, and you're plugged into your Wallytron twenty-four hours a day, red-eyed and unshaven, zapping away like a Wally possessed, while the tempting plateful of turkey burgers and oven chips which the wife brought you three days ago before finally gathering up her belongings and decamping to her mother's, kids and all, lies mouldering disregarded at your elbow. There's no hope for you now. You're beyond all human recall. You're a fully fledged, platinum-plated terminally-fixated Computer Wally ...

But to go back to the games themselves for a moment.

It's surely rather odd that, of the huge number available, so few should relate in any way to the everyday experience of most Wallies. For instance: there are games enabling you to play the role of warlord in a mediaeval Japanese village; there are games in which you battle your way through phantasmagoric mazes, fending off fire-breathing dragons and evil goblins and warlocks. Yet nowhere will you find a game based around the kind of humdrum problems a Computer Wally confronts in his normal daily life – or used to, back in the days when he still had one. The ticklish problem you faced, for example, when you popped round for a housewarming party at your mate Wally's on this vast new Heron Homes estate three miles outside of town, and you clambered into the motor four hours later and it was pitch dark and you couldn't find your way back onto the main road because not only were you stoned out of your brain, but while you'd been busy Getting It Down You, some other Wally had been out and about swapping all the street names round ... Or the time you ran out of petrol in the middle of Windsor Safari Park and you made the wife and Little Wally get out and push, and their legs gave out three hundreds yards from the perimeter fence, and all the time there was this dirty great lion sitting on your bonnet until one of the rangers took a pot shot at it with a tranquillizer dart, only he missed and hit Mrs Wally in the bum instead ...

Enough raw material there for a couple of really magic

computer games, you would have thought. But no. Perhaps until the games people fill this gap in the market, the best solution is for Wallies everywhere to get together and write a few programs of their own, possibly along the following lines:

Spaceshopper
Saturday morning at the Interplanetary hypermarket. Thrills and spills galore as you steer a trolley with three Wallies in it through milling hordes of humanoids doing the weekend shop. You will be enchanted by the smooth Pixel movement of multi-coloured tubs of pot noodles and bumper bog-roll packs as they cascade realistically to the floor all around you.

Scoring
10 points for every pyramid of baked beans tins you plough into.
50 points for sticking one on the manager.
100 points for paying by cheque at a cash-only till.

Yellow Peril
Bank Holiday time on the planet Wally – and it's your mission to transport the wife and kids to a specially designated Wally picnic site by the side of the roaring six-lane Zong-to-Alphamagnon freeway. The trouble is, Mrs Wally's doing the map-reading! Watch out for the fun as she guides you the wrong way round the interstellar one-way system and you're attacked by marauding intergalactic traffic wardens armed with plasma bolts and delayed-action exploding parking tickets.

Computerbore
The ultimate game of skill and tedium for the real computer wizard. See if you can wipe out an entire army of earthlings one by one, by sending them to sleep with a lethal burst of computer jargon. But mind you don't succumb to brain death yourself!

SOME ABSOLUTELY SUPERWALLY PARTIES

The Twenty-First

Something rather magical happens between two and three in the morning at every twenty-first party that there has ever been. Everybody turns into a Wally for the night.

No one is quite sure how or why this phenomenon takes place. Like the irresistible urge to do a Jimmy Durante imitation which overcomes you whenever there's a plastic cup in your hand, it's part of the wonderful natural world of the Wally that scientists have never been able to explain.

So before you go to a twenty-first, it's wise to have some idea what to expect and to prepare accordingly. Usually the scene is something like this:

a) First of all, there's the Wally in the corner, telling very old, very boring Bernard Manning jokes to a sprawling group of

b) Completely paralytic Wallies who lost consciousness soon after the party had started because they'd already spent the first part of the evening Getting One Down them at the Moon and Parrot, because they needed a few drinks before they could face the idea of going to the party of

c) The Wally whose twenty-first it is, and who's standing in the middle of the floor, trying to look as if he's having a wild time, pretending to be drunk and shouting, 'Come on, everybody, let's get on down and dance!' when actually the only two other people on the dance floor are

d) The Wally and Wallette who arrived groping one another, spent the evening in the corner groping one another, and have just decided to go off and grope each other in the upstairs bedroom, unaware that it's already occupied by

e) The Wally who's just met a Wallette on top of a pile of

overcoats on the bed and is trying to get his leg over, while she's saying she's not like that, not here, we've only just met, it's the wrong time of the month, there's somebody's crash helmet sticking into me and anyway I feel really bad about

f) The Wallette who's sitting at the bottom of the stairs crying drunkenly to herself because no one wants to dance with her and her friend's found a feller and is Getting A Bit upstairs and everyone's looking at her and she hates her new job and she knew she shouldn't have come this evening with this bloody great spot which came up this afternoon and her parents keep dropping hints and saying why hasn't she got a boyfriend like all the other girls and she thinks she really might kill herself which would bloody well show them and she's been on the pill for over six months now without even a chance to see if it works or not and tonight the only boy she got to talk to was

g) The Wally who went to the kitchen to get her a drink two and a half hours ago and who never made it because he threw up all over

h) The Wally who was sitting in the kitchen trying to look above it all and thinking how he's going to describe all this in his novel which he hasn't actually started yet but when he does they'll all realise what he was going through when he was interrupted by people being sick on him, not to mention

i) The hairy Wally who has been wandering around with a disgusting looking dog-end in his hand saying to everybody who'll listen, 'Take a hit of this, man, it's absolutely fucking amaaaaaazing stuff, man' until he makes the mistake of saying it to

j) The Wally from next door who's just walked in wearing pyjamas and said that personally he likes to hear kids having a good time but it really is a bit loud, and it is four in the morning, and his wife has a nervous complaint, and the dog's eating the curtains and, fair's fair, lads, some of us have to get up in the morning to do a day's work, you know, so stop this Wallying about NOW.

The Office Leaving Party

No one except a complete Wally could enjoy these occasions – and of course, they offer unlimited opportunities for Wally behaviour.

Ten minutes after the party has started, the resident Office Wally has already tried to open a wine box with a corkscrew, completely flooding the huge bowl of chewy peanuts which is the only food on offer at the party. He has then proceeded to weave his way among the guests with a flagon of Black Label, spilling most of it on the floor and down people's clothes as he goes. And he's told the Personnel Officer that he's always fancied her, even though she's an older woman of course. She in turn has asked him whether he has ever met her husband who's a strong-arm man with a debt-collection agency, and has made a mental note to put a big, red 'WALLY' sticker on his confidential folder first thing the next morning.

Thirty minutes after the party has started, the Wally has belched his way through the boss's speech, and after the presentation to the person who's leaving, he now stands on a table and makes a highly embarrassing impromptu speech in which he announces that the lads have clubbed together for an extra special present, which turns out to be either *The Sex Maniac's Diary* or *How To Be a Wally*, or, if the person is female and leaving to get married, a maternity gown.

An hour and a half after the party has started, everyone has gone home except him and a clutch of other Office Wallies, who now decide to go out, get totally pissed, and then get a bloody great vindaloo down them at the Jewel in the Crown Tandoori House.

The Porn Video Party

All that's needed for a Porn Video Party is a dozen cans of Black Label, a video, a few like-minded Wallies and copies of *I'm Not Feeling Myself Tonight*, *Wham Bam Thank You Ma'am!*, *The Devil in Miss Jones*, *Emmanuelle Meets Lassie*, *The Confessions of a Swedish Virgin Nymphomaniac*, and *Some Came Running*. (Cue for 'Who got hold of this load of old rubbish?' 'Sorry, Wall. Must have got it confused with Paul Raymond's sizzling sextravaganza *Can I Come Again, Please?*')

When, at one in the morning, everyone at the party is either asleep or bored senseless by the spectacle of heaving, spotty Scandinavians Getting a Bit on the screen, one Wally suggests ringing up a few Wallettes and inviting them round for some raunchy late-night fun. They talk about this for an hour, then decide it's a bit too late to ring anyone so they all go home.

The Stag Party

Here is the Wally social occasion par excellence – and yet so many Wallies make the mistake of thinking that all you need for a night to remember is a few of the lads, a table for ten at the local restaurant and a Wallette stripogram artiste.

It's not like that at all. It's impossible to achieve a truly Wally occasion without some careful planning. For the perfect Wally stag night, some – if not all – of the following procedures should be adopted:

  1) Arrive at the restaurant singing, 'Here we are, Here we are, Here we are', and do the conga to your table. At least two members of your party should already have taken their shirts off and should be waving them over their heads like lassoos.

2) If you've booked a table for ten, there should be at least twelve of you. The two spare Wallies should sit in the middle of the table, on other Wallies' laps or at other guests' tables until someone has somehow managed to fit the extra chairs in.

3) Order ten litres of red and white house wine.

4) Throw buns at the other tables. As a couple nearby hurriedly prepare to leave, burst into song with 'One None, One None, One None.'

5) Take as long as possible to order the meal and kick up a fuss if there are no Whopperburgers on the menu. As the waitress serves it up, make leering gestures to the other Wallies behind her back and gasp randily whenever she leans over the table.

6) If there's live music, request 'Stairway to Heaven'. When they say they don't play it, insist that Wally, who's a really brilliant guitarist, is allowed to get on stage to do a couple of numbers. Throw more buns when they refuse.

7) Sing the pornographic versions of *Alouette, Ilkley Moor* and *The Twelve Days of Christmas*, insisting that everyone else in the restaurant joins in.

8) Table-hop and, putting on a serious 'I'm not really pissed' face, ask all the women, particularly the ones that are obviously married, if they fancy you. In the event of other Wallies beating you to it, stand behind them, singing 'Wally's Got a Big One, Wally's Got a Big One' as they try and chat the women up.

9) Do the conga around the restaurant, dragging other guests up from their tables to join the chain. If possible, lead them into the kitchen and emerge all holding your noses.

10) Grab the microphone from the band and make loud farting noises into it.

11) Stand on the table and moon at other guests.

12) Dance with each other between the tables, trip and collapse, giggling, in a pile of chairs, cutlery and broken plates.

13) Throw some wine glasses at the wall. If anyone objects, say you thought it was the custom in

Greek/Russian/French/Indian/English restaurants.

14) At least one Wally should then cut himself badly on the broken glass and be whisked off to hospital in an ambulance, having bled copiously over everyone.

15) Argue for half an hour over the bill.

16) Leave a 15p tip.

17) Leave the restaurant, weaving between the tables, singing 'Cheerio, Cheerio, Cheerio'.

18) Be violently sick on the steps on your way out.

THE WALLY ENTERTAINER

If there's one thing that marks you out straight away as a truly Advanced Wally, it's your burning desire to get up on your hind legs at the office party, pub, social club or annual Club Wally Talent Contest and make a prize tit of yourself in front of a crowd of other Wallies.

There are various ways in which you can do this: you can show them how you can open a beer bottle with your teeth; you can demonstrate how it's possible to shatter the bottom off a beer bottle by bringing your hand down sharply on the top; you can wow them with the old Clint Eastwood trick of striking a match on your zipper ... But experience shows that there's nothing tickles an audience of Wallies quite as much as when you treat them to your impressions of a few boring old Superwally Celebrities. Try it: they'll split their sides. Alternatively they could just split to the bar. Or pelt you with peanuts and beer cans. Still, as they say, that's showbiz.

A word or two first about technique. The success of any comedy act depends greatly on *timing*, but there's no need to make a fetish of it. As far as a brief comic turn in the saloon bar of the Moon and Parrot goes, any time after six will do. In fact, you could probably give a one-man rendering of the death of Little Nell and there still wouldn't be a dry seat in the house.

Bruce Forsyth

Always a favourite with the punters.

1) Lift right leg, holding it bent at knee. Place knuckles of right hand against forehead:

2) Arrange features in grinning rictus, jutting chin forward as if trying to swallow tip of nose with lower lip:

3) Mince forward to footlights, jerking head back and forth like a turkey. Pause to acknowledge screams of mirth, shouts of GERROFF, WHADDA LOADA RUBBISH etc.

4) Knock them dead with a typical bellybusting Brucie catchphrase, e.g.:

GOOD GAME GOOD GAME

DIDN'T THEY DO WELL *or*

NICE TER SEE YER TER SEE YER …

5) Fling arms forward and *up*:

… NIIIII-CE!

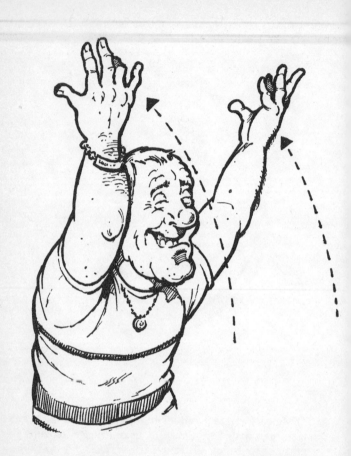

So far so good. Your audience is really falling about at this mesmeric display of top-flight impressionistic skill. You may even find that there's a bit of a hiatus here while the smelling salts are passed around and the stretcher cases removed. So before the rest of the audience have a chance to hotfoot it to the Gents or nearest exit, whip out the old beret and belted mackintosh and hit them with another surefire crowd-pleaser, viz. your patent ...

Frank Spenser impression

Another guaranteed winner – and so easy too, given your natural affinity with the role.

1) Pull down beret well over ears.
2) Suck in cheeks; purse lips into pouting 'O' shape. Adopt startled, vaguely indignant expression.

3) Puff out chest; plant right hand on hip; swivel head around gormlessly.
4) Bring the house down with:
MMMM ... NICE
OOOOOH ... BETTEEEEEE
or
DA DONKEE'S DONE A LIDDEL WHOOPSIE IN DA CORRIDOR

By now there should be total pandemonium out there. They're just wetting themselves. But the fun isn't over yet – not by a long way. There's still Tommy Cooper, Ken Dodd, Larry Grayson and the entire cast of Hi-De-Hi to come, not to mention your grand finale: the bit you copied off Mike Yarwood, where you stuff a ping pong ball in cheek, clamber on top of a bar stool and do an impression of Max Bygraves doing an impression of Michael Foot doing an impression of a dead ostrich singing *You Are My Sunshine* while drinking from a can of Red Stripe ...

Unfortunately what usually happens at this point is that either the Wallies at the back start a slow-handclap, or else the mike is suddenly snatched out of your hand and you find yourself being hustled off stage to make way for some amateur topless go-go dancer, budding Paul Daniels or a blowsy half-sozzled middle-aged Wallette who insists on favouring the assembled company with a selection from *South Pacific*. And the curious thing is, *they* always get a standing ovation. Still, it just highlights one of the problems you face when you perform for Wallies: they just don't know sheer class when it's handed to them on a plate.

THE WALLY COUNTRY CODE

Most people think of the average Wally as a confirmed city-dweller: the type who'd no more dream of escaping to the country in search of pastoral peace and mystic one-ness with Nature than he would of joining MENSA, becoming a Community Service Volunteer, or taking out life-membership of the National Trust. And for ninety-nine per cent of the year, that's probably the case.

And yet from time to time there comes a moment in every Wally's life when he begins to tire of the choking traffic fumes and all the din and confusion of modern city life; when the pleasure of kicking an empty Macdonald's carton up and down a shopping precinct, endlessly doing Kerb Endo's on Little Wally's BMX bike, or gobbing out of car windows at passing pedestrians begins to pall. When, frankly, urban life, with all the splendid opportunities it affords for being a complete and utter Wally, is about as appealing as a three-day-old reheated Chinese Take Away.

At such moments, even the most dedicated Wally feels a vague hankering for something completely different. He yearns for the green fields, the clear blue skies, the wide open spaces. He longs to hear the birds singing in the treetops, the soft, soothing rustle of a gentle summer breeze and the refreshing babble of a nearby brook ...

And so, once or twice a year, usually around Bank Holiday time, he loads up the motor with a primus stove, insulated plastic picnic box, twelve cans of Black Label and a giant ghetto blaster and, accompanied by thousands of other Wallies all of whom have experienced exactly the same lemming-like urge, he bids farewell to the city and heads off to the country to lay waste to that instead.

Top Ten Wally Ways to Commune with Nature

Given the appalling lack of really gross Wally pubs in rural areas and the fact that the slightest error in map-reading is liable to land you in the middle of nowhere, miles from the nearest Kentucky and with not a Mecca Entertainments Complex in sight, you might think that opportunities for being a Wally in the countryside are pretty few and far between. Not so. The openings are there *if* you're prepared to look for them. Here are a few suggestion to start you off:

1) Dig up an ancient Druid burial mound on the off-chance of finding a Cadbury-Schweppes Golden Egg at the bottom of it.

2) Attempt to establish an instant rapport with every farm animal in sight by blowing up its nose the Woodhouse way.

3) Swarm into a remote country pub with a crowd of other Wallies and loon around in the snug, doing Walter Gabriel impressions, slopping beer all over the locals and blowing up their nose the Woodhouse way.

4) Select a field criss-crossed with high-voltage electricity cables and steer your radio-controlled Mini Piper Cherokee smack into them.

5) Pick off anything that moves with an air rifle.

6) Get pissed and sit down in a cowpat.

7) Plunder the hedgerows, uprooting wild flowers and sprigs of cow parsley to stick on the front of your motor.

8) Check whether those hours of obedience-training in the park have paid off by letting the Alsatian loose in a field of sheep and ordering it to SIIIIII-*T*.

9) Using a picnic tablecloth, perform a mock-bullfight with the cow in the nextdoor field, then …

10) Discover it's not a cow after all.

WALLY CULTURE

If ever there was proof that the influence of Superwallies in high places is a power for good in this great country of ours, it's the truly heartening rise of Wally Culture.

FACT

We're now exporting more boring old totally non-Wally works of art to gullible American museums than ever before, so that there's more room in our stately homes for frisbee parks, funfairs and dolphinariums.

FACT

The government is very sensibly cutting grants to time-wasting and noisy so-called fringe theatre companies, so that instead of staging hysterical playlets about Soweto, pubs can once more use their upstairs rooms for profitable and worthwhile purposes: snooker, aerobics classes, mud-wrestling and so on.

FACT

The only plays running in the West End are now exclusively written by, acted by, and performed for Wallies. Classics like *No Sex Please, We're Wallies, The Real Wally* and *Wally Pulls it Off* are playing to packed houses of delighted Wallies, as well as coachloads of bewildered foreigners anxious to discover why London is now renowned as the home of Wally theatre.

So pervasive is the influence of Wally Culture that many of our top playwrights are actually revising earlier work in order to keep pace with the times. Possibly the most successful revison was by Harold Pinter, who chucked out all his pre-Wally rubbish and replaced it with such classics as *Wally Comes Home*:

<u>A Wally</u>: It's a bloody choker, it is.

<u>Another Wally</u>: Right.

<u>They stare at the audience for several minutes.</u>

<u>A Wally</u>: A bloody choker.

<u>Another Wally</u>: This is it.

<u>They stare at the audience for several minutes.</u>

<u>Another Wally</u>: When would that be then?

<u>A Wally</u>: Eh?

<u>Another Wally</u>: I said when would that be?

<u>They stare at the audience for several minutes.</u>

<u>A Wally</u>: What were you talking about.

<u>Another Wally</u>: When?

<u>A Wally</u>: Just then. You said 'When would that
be then?' I heard it quite distinctly. I've
got a good memory for that sort of thing.
'When would that be?' you said. I didn't
understand. You lost me.

<u>Another Wally</u>: Oh. I meant, 'When did you
choke her?'

<u>A Wally</u>: When did I choke who?

<u>Another Wally</u>: Her, you Wally. I heard you
say it. You said you'd bloody choke her. It
sounded interesting. Different. Not the sort
of thing you hear every day. People don't talk
about choking each other every day. They talk
about being cheesed off about things. Browned

off. The wife doesn't understand me. Gets on my wick. Gets my dander up. That sort of thing. But not 'I'm going to bloody choke her'. Not often anyway.

<u>A Wally</u>: No, I suppose not. I don't know. I'm confused now. I wasn't. Confused, that is. But I am now. I never knew I had a wife.

<u>They both stare at the audience for several minutes.</u>

<u>End of Act I</u>

Wally Shakespeare

It's an enterprise that has grabbed the imagination of Wally educationalists from Milton Keynes to Leighton Buzzard: the complete rewriting of the works of Shakespeare, so that, instead of being in unintelligible and totally old-fashioned English which, let's face it, no one speaks these days, the Bard's great masterpieces will be translated into so-called 'Wallyspeak' and so be made accessible to Wallies everywhere.

The person behind the idea is none other than Dr Dick Wally, the Leicester University academic whose Wally version of Hamlet's 'To be or not to be/That is the question' speech ('To go for the big one or not to go for the big one/At the end of the day that's basically what it's all about') was widely praised.

Here then are two versions of Act IV Scene 7 of *Henry V* – the boring, old original version and the exciting new, Dick Wally version:

WILLIAM SHAKESPEARE

K. Hen: I was not angry since I came to France
Until this instant. Take a trumpet, herald;
Ride thou unto the horseman on yon hill;
If they will fight with us, bid them come down,
Or void the field; they do offend our sight......

WALLY SHAKESPEARE

K. Hen: I kid you not, I'm as sick as a bloody parrot. In my book, the Frogs are way out of order on this one. It's on yer bike time - bloody shit or get off the pot, if you'll pardon my French. And we won't be pardoning theirs - ber-boom!

75

Exeter: Here comes the herald of the French, my liege.

Gloucester: His eyes are humbler than they us'd to be.

K. Hen: How now! What means this, herald? know'st thou not
That I have fin'd these bones of mine for ransom?
Com'st thou again for ransom?

Exeter: Say no more, Hen. Talk of the devil - here he comes now.

Gloucester: No way is that one happy Frenchman.

K. Hen: Hop off, you Frogs.

Sounds Wally

These days, an awful lot of Wallies still seem to think that when it comes to music, you can't beat a blast of Frankie Goes to Hollywood, Kajagoogoo, or, if you're into Heavy Metal, the latest single from Motorhead – which is fine if you've got Heinz Vegetable Salad where your brains used to be and you happen to thrill to the sound of a million crashing dustbin lids and pneumatic road drills (and of course, you do).

But ever since the LSO made their successful bid for Wally credibility by throwing together a hotch-potch of classical numbers, slapping on a disco beat and releasing it as a chart-topping 45, a lot of today's more advanced and sophisticated Wallies have realized that to get ahead of the pack, sound-wise, you have to go one better: you have to get switched on to the Classics too.

What – Beethoven? Tchaikovsky? Stuff like that? Leave it out ...

Okay. Admittedly you can't always pogo or break-dance to them, but some of those evergreen classical sounds are terrific for headbanging, and anyway, even if you never actually play them, a couple of classical albums can look pretty impressive peeking out from among the Duran Duran singles and Mum's TV theme-tune compilations.

But supposing you're pig-ignorant about classical music? Supposing you thought that Handel's Largo came in cans? Where do you start?

No problem.

Because nowadays all an Advanced Wally has to do to get himself a reputation for genuine musical taste and discernment is to cut along to the local Boots or John Menzies and check out

THE WALLYDISC CLASSICS FOR PLEASURE COLLECTION

Now, a lot of the sleeve-notes on the more upmarket classical labels can be a bit unhelpful, not to say intimidating for the novice. For instance, does any Wally seriously want to know that Bach wrote his famous Air on a

Slim Panatella in the year sixteen-whatever-it-was in response to a commission from the Kapellmeister of the Leipzig-a-Go-Go Discorama? Or that Mozart's Concerto for Colonel Bogey Car Horn was first performed by Wolfgang and the lads while they were Getting One Down them in the back of a coach in a lay-by on the Salzburg by-pass?

No. What you're interested in is the music: what to play, when to play it, and how to pass the time while you're pretending to listen to it. So with this in mind, Wallydisc have prepared their own Classical Hit Parade, plus a few helpful tips designed to maximise your listening pleasure.

Top Ten Wallydisc Classical Pops of All Time

1) *Tchaikovsky: the Dance of the Sugar-Plum Fairy*
   Light, fluffy and tinkling. Play it as you prance round the lounge in your new Adidas trainers.

2) *Ravel's Bolero*
   Perfect Saturday night leg-over music. Or of course you can ice-skate to it ...

3) *Richard Strauss: Thus Spake Zarathustra*
   That's the 2001 theme to you. Beat time with a rolled copy of *Smash Hits* or scrape away at an imaginary violin.

4) *Rachmaninov: Rhapsody on a Theme of Paganini*
   Watch out for the slushy bit that goes da da-da-da-da *dum dum* ... One for the Mums and Dads.

5) *Mendelssohn: Fingal's Cave*
   Very boring. Nothing much you can do with this except sit down and listen to it.

6) *Tchaikovsky: Swan Lake*
   To remind you of the time you nearly bagged one with Little Wally's air rifle.

7) *Rimsky-Korsakov; the Flight of the Bumble Bee*
   To remind you of the time you nearly bagged Little Wally with Little Wally's air rifle.

8) *Chopin: Preludes*
   Moody and soulful. Have a good blub to it after watching the lads get hammered Five Nothing in the EUFA Cup qualifier.

9) *Tchaikovsky: 1812 Overture*
World War Three erupts in your own living room. Just the job for Lads' Night, Cup Final Night, or breaking the furniture at parties.

10) *Beethoven's Choral Symphony*
Heavy but fun. Play it full-volume on the car stereo. It'll give a whole new meaning to the Sound of Happy Motoring.

The Wally Walkman

POLITICS: THE ART OF THE SUPERWALLY

In no sphere of modern life is the rise and rise of the Superwally more evident and noticeable than the world of politics.

The time when politicians merely needed to be neatly dressed, well connected and at least semi-literate is truly dead and gone. Now that Wallies form such an important and growing part not only of the electorate itself but also of the media, the only way to the top of the greasy pole is for every politician to try and prove to the world that he is a bigger Wally or Wallette than his or her opponent.

Not surprisingly, this trend started in America. The experts are divided as to who precisely was the first leading American politican to show that, if you can prove to the nation that you are unquestionably a Superwally, then power and success will soon be within your grasp. Some say it was Lyndon Johnson picking his beagle up by the ears for the television cameras; others that it was Gerald Ford falling down the steps of Airforce One. Then there was George McGovern crying like a Wally, Edward Kennedy driving like a Wally, and Jimmy Carter collapsing in the middle of a fun run in a spectacularly Wally way – all culminating in the moment when the man who has truly given the term 'Superwally' international significance ambled photogenically into the White House four years ago.

Not that we in Britain have lagged behind. No one could argue that the country that has produced men of the stature of George Brown, Sir Alec Douglas-Home, Edward Heath and Cyril Smith has failed to keep pace with the world development of Superwallies in politics over the last twenty years.

These days, politicians everywhere are recognizing that the so-called Wally Factor is an important part of their public image and are now working on new techniques to show the voters what complete and utter Wallies they all are.

Among the more successful methods are:

The Skinner Skinhead

Now very popular among backbench MPs who like to see their names in the papers, this method involves jumping up and down in the House of Commons, shouting, swearing, going red in the face and calling everyone a bloody liar until eventually the Speaker shows you the red card. Dennis Skinner, the original Skinhead, is now regarded as the Wally To Watch on the Labour backbenches.

The Williams Wobble

A simple device for winning affection and easy laughs, the Williams Wobble involves missing every important train by at least five minutes and always arriving late and breathless for interviews. Shirley Williams, who created this technique, applied it to perfection when she managed to arrive too late to catch a launch which was to carry the SDP leaders down the Thames as part of a campaign to establish them as the party of efficiency and unity.

The Parkinson Peccadillo

A tricky manoeuvre for all but the most adept Wallies, the Parkinson Peccadillo involves looking like Mr Clean, being widely tipped as a future prime minister, getting caught with your trousers down and then being brought back to public life as the saviour of the government after a *Daily Mail* campaign. After all, any old Wally can make a mistake, can't he?

The Hailsham Dotty Old Peer Routine

Perfected over many years as a Superwally, the Hailsham Dotty Old Peer Routine involves behaving like an ageing Billy Bunter on speed, making fatuous remarks about anything that takes your fancy, losing your temper for absolutely no reason and wearing silly hats when there are cameras about.

The Howe Amiable Bungle
Invented by the well-known Conservative foreign secretary, this technique involves shuffling around looking embarrassed, talking in a funereal monotone normally reserved for Speak-Your-Weight machines, blinking a lot when interviewed and losing your trousers on a train carrying every political journalist in the country.

TRUE CONFESSIONS

No Superwally likes to feel totally uninformed about what's going on in the world around him. While the mere Wally may be proud of his ignorance and work daily to increase it, the Superwally will tirelessly keep up with the news that matters – politics, the economy, the Embassy World Snooker Championships, and how busty Page Three Girl Katrina has big plans to be an actress (and we're sure you'll agree she's got great prospects before her!)

So he reads the soaraway *Sun*.

The most memorable item for *Sun* Superwallies in recent times (apart from 'RANDY ANDY'S HANKY SPANKY!', 'BASTARD! *Sun* readers blast "Adolf" Scargill', and "EMERY WAS FLOP IN BED", says Dick's frilly-knicker sex siren') was the news that Wallies all over the country were to be given the chance to confess their crimes to their favourite newspaper. But although several major unsolved cases were cleared up this way, there were several Wally confessions that were considered too shocking, even for *Sun* readers ...

'I slept with our sixteen-year-old babysitter'

'I just can't think what came over me. I'm a happily married man with a gorgeous wife, two lovely kids and a nice home, but I once did something that has kept me awake at nights just thinking about it.

'It was when the kids were quite young. The wife and I went out to a party and I suppose the truth is that I'd had one or two too many. I offered to take our young babysitter, an attractive, curvaceous sixteen-year-old called Barbara back to her home. Her parents were away and she asked me if I'd like to come in for a quick cup of tea. Well, one thing led to another and, by the end of the first cup, I was pretty sure that this young girl was eager for a sizzling sex session with me on the settee. Unfortunately I was so pissed that, before I could even suggest a quick one, I passed out on the floor. My wife has always been suspicious about why I came back so late that night, but I've never been able to tell her the full story.

'Now I can't sleep at night for thinking that Busty Barbara, the sexy schoolgirl siren of the baby-sitting circle, could have been mine for the night. But just telling the soaraway *Sun* makes me feel better already!'

Terry, Luton

'It was just a lark for us – but seventeen cars, a couple of innocent bystanders and a mongrel puppy paid a terrible price.'

'I was out with a couple of the lads, and we thought it would be a bit of a giggle if we turned round some traffic diversion signs so that a few motors would be sent round the one-way system in our town the wrong way. Well, it worked a treat – not even the ambulances could get through the debris. Then we smashed a few windows, nutted someone who was winding us up by looking at us, nutted someone else who was winding us up by refusing to look at us, tipped up a milk float and attached a banger to a dog's tail to see what would happen. Then we booked a punter for a flagrant double yellow line traffic violation and went back to the station.

'The sarge said it was a good day's work, but I've always had a nagging feeling that what we did wasn't quite right.'

PC Trevor, Derby

'I'm a spoilt Wally Hooray and I love every minute of it'

'I've always felt rather awful about spending public money wining and dining a string of randy models, prancing about naked with Vicki Hodge on the sun-drenched island of Mustique, getting spanked by topless waitresses in suspender belts, asking Selina Scott if she'd like to come round the back of the studio in the middle of an interview, and, the only time I was asked to do anything remotely serious, spraying journalists with white paint and then braying with laughter. I read the *Sun* every day and love all the bits I can understand. My head hurts now so I'd better stop.'

Darren, Buckingham Palace, London

'I Got One Down me what I shouldn't of'

'I told my mate I got 795 on the Asteroids at the Moon and Parrot when I'd really only got 10. He only managed to get 5 so he had to buy me a pint.'

Pete, Newcastle

'Could my boyish prank have changed the course of modern history?'

'I'm in my fifties now, but I feel very bad about something that happened when I was a 'slip of a lad' back in 1963. I was on holiday in America staying with these friends in Texas. The son of the family was called Mitch, and we lads used to go to nearby Dallas with a rifle – there was an old warehouse there and we used to shoot beer cans off a roof over the other side of the road. One fateful day, there were a lot of people milling about on the street below. We'd had a bit to drink, and when it came to my shot, I tripped and shot down into the street instead of across it. I may be wrong, but I thought I saw someone in an open-top limousine fall down as he was waving to a friend. I hope and pray I'm wrong, but I've always been haunted by the thought that our silly prank may have had serious consequences.'

Ginger, Tonbridge Wells

THE INNER WALLY

Wallies have psychological crises in their lives just like anyone else – and it's no use their family and friends saying, 'Wally's just being a bigger Wally than he normally is' and thinking that the problem will go away. Someone suffering in this way needs to be nursed through the dark clouds of gloom, depression and self-doubt to the sunny skies beyond, so that they can be the familiar carefree Wally that you knew of old.

Above all, remember that psychological crises can be serious. In some cases, days of introspection, worry and guilt can cause such a radical transformation of character that, by the end of it all, the sufferer is a Wally in name only.

Following recent violent incidents caused by Spurs and Chelsea Wallies in Europe, the government commissioned a report by a team of psychologists, whose brief was to study in detail the Wally lifestyle and Wally habits and behaviour. At the time many people were puzzled by the move: after all, why should a series of perfectly healthy Wally incidents, only marred by a typically cynical over-reaction by foreign policemen using incredible violence to break up quite innocent looting parties, be thought to require an investigation into so-called hang-ups and problems? The only explanation was that the growing Wally faction in Whitehall (see *Politics: the Art of the Superwally*) must have been behind it all.

Yet the experts' findings did, after all, have some relevance. They concluded that the average Wally experiences what they call The Five Crises in his life. So here is a brief account of how each of those crises feels to the Wally, with appropriate remedies:

Crisis One: Childhood

At the age of about seven, a conflict within Little Wally's subconscious comes to boiling-point. On one side, he's feeling, 'I don't really *want* to pull down saplings in the park and have swordfights with the other little Wallies like in *Robin of Sherwood*. I'd like to stay at home, read a book, listen to some early Chopin preludes and learn the rudiments of chess.'

Meanwhile, the other side of his subconscious is telling him: 'Leave it out, Wally. If Dad wanted to have a little ponce sitting at home playing with his rudiments, he'd have had a little girl, wouldn't he? So on yer bike, my son, and you're the sheriff.'

Solution: Promise the little brat an A-team sweat shirt if he swears never to look at another book. Then lock up the nancy-boy classical records, with the possible exception of *Hooked on Classics* and *Cats*.

Crisis Two: Adolescence

The Wally has reached a stage in his life when he's beginning to have trouble with girls. The problem is, he likes them. He dreams of having conversations and meaningful relationships with them, and makes secret plans for a long weekend in Paris in the hope of finally meeting the girl of his dreams. He tries hard to join in with the other Wallies and say, 'Gor, catch a load of that' whenever he sees a girl go by in a tight T-shirt, but, in his heart of hearts, he'd like to go up to her and say something sweet and understanding that will show her he's not like all the other boys.

Solution: Find a Wallette who's not likely to fall for all this Mills and Boon slop. Make it worth her while – promise her a Radio One biro or something – and get her to take him round the back of the Moon and Parrot for a quick knee-trembler. When she rejoins the other Wallettes at the bar, she should make loud references to Wee Willie Winkie.

As everyone in the pub rocks with laughter, his attitude towards women will improve immediately.

Crisis Three: Fatherhood

The Wally looks back on his life so far and, for a moment, it seems to him a desolate wasteland of empty beer-cans, smashed supermarket trollies, inflated condoms and cheap motor accessories, all signifying very little. Then he looks at Little Wally as he puts the finishing touches to a spring trap which will catapult the neighbour's ginger cat fifty feet in the air the next time it sets foot in the back yard, and he wonders whether he shouldn't be showing him a better way forward – perhaps the occasional book, a chess set, or a recording of *Chopin's Greatest Hits* on Classics for Pleasure.

Solution: Try it. After killing the neighbour's cat, Little Wally will use the chess pieces for target practice with his air rifle and the record as a frisbee. Face it – being a complete and utter Wally is in the blood and nothing's going to shift it.

Crisis Four: Middle Age

The years are beginning to take their toll on the Wally. He'd prefer to watch *Crossroads* than spend the evening Getting a Few Down him at the Moon and Parrot. And, even when he is out with the lads, he feels a bit queasy after his ninth pint. It doesn't feel right playing football with a beercan in the car park any more and, at the Christmas party, when the Office Wallette suggests their annual visit to the firm's store-room to check stock-levels, his heart sinks and he cries off, claiming that Mrs Wally was suspicious last Christmas when she found wood shavings in his Y-fronts. He watches *The Price is Right* every week, but even that makes him feel a bit tired. Frankly, life's a bit of a choker these days.

Solution: There's basically no solution to the Wally's mid-life crisis, beyond accepting the fact that only people like Patrick Moore and Ted Rogers can manage to be complete and utter Wallies all their lives — and even that took them years of practice.

Crisis Five: Old Age

What good is a Wally who can hardly lift a can of Black Label, let alone Get It Down him? Who's such a menace on the roads that no one lets him near his old Escort, which is gathering dust in the garage? Who gets jostled down at the Moon and Parrot by a new generation of Wallies not interested in his Wally tales of yore: the day we got to the Membury service station in $22\frac{1}{2}$ minutes flat; the day we gave the Wallette behind the bar a vibrator and she thought it was for curling her hair; the day we saw the late, great Dickie Davies at the local darts championship and I asked him ... Leave it out, Grandad, Wally tales of yawn, more like, eh lads?

Solution: Apart from filling up his time with totally useless activities (See *Occupational Therapy for the Elderly Wally*), there's sadly not much that can be done for this decrepit old Wally as he shuffles his way towards the front of the queue for the Great Shopping Precinct in the sky.

OCCUPATIONAL THERAPY
FOR THE ELDERLY WALLY

Just because the Elderly Wally doesn't rush about in the way he used to, there's no reason to think that he can't pursue Wally activities in his own quiet, utterly senile way. Try some of these occupational exercises to keep him more or less alert and fill in those long, empty hours between *Crossroads* episodes:

1) Attach a Woolworth's Old Folks' Home Head-Banger to the back of his armchair. Whenever an old Status Quo number comes up on one of Golden Oldies slots on the radio, he can pull it round in front of him and hammer his grizzled old head against the cushioned board just like when he was a lad.

2) Give him some motor accessories that you've picked up cheap from a bric-a-brac shop and get him to fix them on his wheelchair. It'll take him days to fit the Go-Faster stripes, Radio 2 sun vizor, nodding dog, roll bar and Colonel Bogey hooter. Once he's done it, tell him not to be such a silly old fool and that he'd better dismantle it all before he gets too excited.

3) Get him to crochet a cover for next door's Cortina. When he's finished that, tell him that the caravan could do with one too.

4) Buy him five hundred large boxes of matches and tell him to get on with building a matchstick model of Blackpool pier, the Hammersmith Palais, the Kop or the Taj Mahal. (No, not the new Indian restaurant on the High Street, you silly old goat, the famous wonder of the world.)

5) Encourage him to develop an intimate daily relationship with the television newsreaders. Hardly a

day will go by without the old Wally puzzling over such questions as:

- What Jan Leeming's done with her hair tonight
- Whether Alastair Burnett has grown snootier to the other readers since he got his knighthood
- Why Carol Barnes always reaches for a glass of water so eagerly at the end of the news
- Whether it's really water
- If Andrew Gardner is just saying, 'Well done, lass,' to Tina Jenkins when they dim the lights at the end of news, or if he's asking her whether she fancies getting the hell out of this dump, going to a disco in Mayfair, bopping to the wee small hours and then back to his place to go over the main points again?

WHAT TO DO
WITH A DEAD WALLY'S ASHES

No Wally would like to think that he'll be completely forgotten after he's Gone for the Big One for positively the last time. Not for him a dignified burial in the peaceful country churchyard where the bones of his ancestors have lain for generations. Even in death, he wants to be where the action is.

So as well as clubbing together to buy some fitting memorial to him – a park bench for other Wallies to tip up and scratch their names on, say, or a commemorative trough in the Gents at Stamford Bridge – his grieving relatives should make sure that Wally's mortal remains are preserved in the quiet, tasteful way he would have liked.

Choosing a suitable final resting place for your Dear Departed is bound to be a painful and harrowing task, but here are a few suggestions:

● In an engraved tankard behind the bar at the Moon and Parrot
● On the starting grid at Brands Hatch
● In his best mate Wally's petrol tank ('Good old Wally – bloody joker to the last')
● In a coffee jar in the lounge

This last idea was in fact popularized by none other than Superwallette Fay Hiller, Dick Emery's frilly-knicker sex siren, who revealed that she had stolen some of the zany comedian's mortal remains after the cremation and now keeps them in a love-shrine in her sitting room. (Most Wally families should probably avoid this, for fear of serving up cups of Wally in mistake for Maxwell House at the monthly Ann Summers Sex Accessory coffee morning.)

Top Ten Wally ways of trying to raise money for a Kidney Machine

1 Sitting on a pavement from the 10th December to the 1st January in a bid to beat the world record for queueing for the January sales.
2 Getting a leg amputated and hopping from Land's End to John O'Groats.
3 Talking for over sixty hours without a break to David Hamilton and suffering permanent brain damage as a result.
4 Getting sponsored for the London Marathon and collapsing after half a mile.
5 Going up to someone and saying, 'I'm collecting money for a kidney machine or something, give us some'.
6 Collecting 100,000 beer tops and then discovering that they should have been milk bottle tops instead.
7 Going on a sponsored pub crawl where the sponsor had to buy all the drinks.
8 Phoning in a pledge of £100 to Terry Wogan's BBC Telethon and then realising that you're meant to *collect* £100, not give it away.
9 Trying to run the full length of the Great North Road attached to a kidney machine.
10 Getting buried fifty feet under the ground for a month by which time everyone has forgotten all about you.

Top Ten Wally Conversational Topics

1 Dick Emery's amazing showgirl love-nest shock secret.
2 Whether Torvil and Dean are just good friends or whether he gives her the occasional Triple Lutz in the dressing room after the show.
3 Which of the Coronation Street cast will be the next to die, get busted, or be caught with his pants down.
4 Our Boys in Blue, God Bless 'Em.
5 This new government bill to stop poofs from molesting innocent police officers who from time to time in the normal exercise of their duties quite understandably wander into notorious Soho gay bars dressed in black leather and hang around waiting for some pervert to sidle up to them and suggest a bit of hanky-panky in the Gents.
6 The latest totally unjustifiable attempt by some limp-wristed bloody Leftie in the Home Office to prevent the National Front from exercising their inalienable democratic right to march down the local High Street, smash up an Asian deli or two and knock a few nignogs' heads together.
7 The latest vicious and totally unjustifiable prison sentences meted out to a few high-spirited British lads who went over to Luxembourg for the Big One and got a bit carried away I grant you.
8 The latest shock-horror rapist scare and what you'd like to do if you ever got your hands on the bastard responsible mind you if you want my opinion any girl who's out on her own at that time of night is bloody well asking for trouble.
9 The case for reviving the good old mediaeval practice of hanging, drawing and quartering then carrying the victim's head through the streets of London on a pole, and how personally you're not a violent man but when you see the kind of crimes people commit nowadays you'd be only too happy to do the job yourself.
10 Who Ernie will get to replace Eric.

Top Ten Wally Bodily Ailments

1 Jogger's Nipple
2 Medallion Rash
3 Saturday Night Fever
4 Docker's Armpit
5 Brewer's Droop
6 Cauliflower Ear
7 Double vision
8 Chronic flatulence
9 Acne
10 Undescended testicles

Top Ten Wallies who Went for The Big One but found themselves in All Sorts Of Trouble when The Chips Were Down

1 The Wally who tried to row the Atlantic in a four-foot boat. (He made it.)
2 The Wally waitress who gave Prince Andrew a spanking. (Her boss grabbed all the publicity.)
3 The Wally on the *Mail On Sunday* who thought that flying a mangy Libyan rabbit back from Tripoli and headlining the story 'HONEYBUN'S HOME' would increase circulation. (It did.)
4 The double-barrelled Wally who set out to walk to the North Pole, then had to be airlifted home a couple of days later suffering from frostbite and a sprained ankle. (He succeeded on his next attempt.)
5 The Wally who jumped off Clifton Suspension Bridge dressed up as Santa Claus with an elastic band round his waist. (He should have done it in the nude.)
6 The Wally Cambridge Cox who thought he was in the high hurdles and steered the boat into Hammersmith Bridge. (He made the whole dull old sporting ritual worth watching for a change.)
7 The Wally Test Match streaker who dashed across the pitch waving his arms and brought all play to a standstill. (He forgot to remove his Y-fronts.)
8 The two Danish Wallies who had a few too many and sawed the arm off the Little Mermaid. (They brought it back the next morning.)
9 The protesting Greenpeace Wallies who shinned up Big Ben and draped a couple of banners over it to draw attention to the government's policy on nuclear waste. (They should have done it just for a lark.)
10 The Wally newspaper editor who sued the BBC's *Week Ending* programme for describing him as a brainless yobbo. (He should have taken it as a compliment.)

Top Ten Wally things to do with a Football Scarf

1 Tie it to the car aerial as you drive off with a load of other Wallies to see the Big One at Stamford Bridge.
2 Chase after other Wallies at a motorway service station, whirling it round your head, making silly whooping noises and pretending it's a lassoo.
3 Stuff it down the front of your trousers and jerk your pelvis lasciviously at female passers-by.
4 Drop your trousers, wrap it round your waist and mince up and down on top of a table like a model in a mini-skirt.
5 Use it as a boxing glove as you hammer the fruit machine in a pathetic attempt to make it cough up some money.
6 Have a tug of war with it over one of the partitions in the Gents.
7 Be sick into it.
8 Get confused in your drunken excitement at the match and throw it on to the pitch thinking it's a toilet roll.
9 Pretend to hang yourself with it after the boys got well and truly stuffed Five Nothing at Stamford Bridge.
10 Succeed.

Top Ten Wally Football Clubs

1 Chelsea
2 Birmingham
3 Millwall
4 Celtic
5 Wolves
6 Grimsby Town
7 Luton
8 Mönchengladbach
9 Manchester City
10 Leyton Orient

Top Ten Wally Newspaper Columns

1 Queen of the Box Nina Myskow's Wally of the Week.
2 Straight Talk by Plain John Smith.
3 Claude Duval, the Punter's Pal.
4 Roderick Mann, the Man the Stars Talk To.
5 Stafford Hildren, The Man Inside your Telly.
6 Godfrey Smith.
7 Me and My Mum.
8 Joe Ashton, the Voice of the People.
9 Dear Unity's Advice Straight From The Heart.
10 Felicity Hawkins' Soap People.

Top Ten Wally Sports

1 Snooker
2 Darts
3 Windsurfing
4 Playing football with a beer can
5 Parascending
6 Motocross
7 Ice-skating
8 Matchplay bowls
10 Rally driving

Top Ten Wally Careers

1 Stripping vicar
2 Policeman
3 Radio One disc jockey
4 Doorstep aluminium double-glazing salesman
5 Professional ballroom-dancer
6 Minister for Drought
7 Motorcycle stunt-rider
8 The SAS
9 Professional lookalike
10 Human cannonball

1 The two Wallies in *The Professionals* do all their own stunts.
2 *The Thornbirds* was filmed on location in the Australian outback.
3 Ninety per cent of road accidents are caused by people driving too slowly.
4 England would have the best football team in the world if they just had a striker of the class of Platini.
5 All Oriental women have crooked vaginas.
6 Mrs Thatcher is an ordinary housewife and mother.
7 Boy George is not just a pretty face.
8 Your No. 1 *Sun* is the only paper that gives you a true picture of what's really going on.
9 Christmas is for the kids.
10 The British Rail 24-Hour Breakfast is *not* so called because it was cooked 24 hours before you get to eat it.

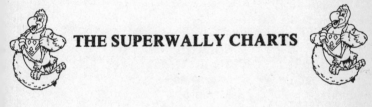

THE SUPERWALLY CHARTS

1 The Barron Knights
2 Status Quo
3 The Bee Gees
4 Bananarama
5 Marillion
6 Instant Sunshine
7 The King's Singers
8 The Nolan Sisters
9 Queen
10 Sky

1 Barry Manilow
2 Max Bygraves
3 Shakin' Stevens
4 Julio Iglesias (except when he's singing with Willy Nelson)
5 Richard Clayderman
6 Rod Stewart
7 Demis Roussos
8 Any chat show host who tries to sing (particularly Des O'Connor and Bob Monkhouse)
9 Lena Zavaroni
10 Neil

1 Jim Davison
2 Little and Large
3 Marti Caine
4 Bernard Manning
5 Bruce Forsyth
6 Cannon and Ball
7 Terry Scott
8 Max Bygraves
9 Jimmy Tarbuck
10 Tim Brooke-Taylor

1 Jeremy Beadle
2 David Vine
3 Leslie Crowther
4 Jonathan King
5 Barry Took
6 Kenny Everett
7 Kenny Lynch
8 Russell Grant
9 Max Bygraves
10 Jimmy Savile

1 Joan Collins
2 Victoria Principal
3 Prince Andrew
4 Elizabeth Taylor
5 David Frost
6 Omar Sharif
7 Ronald Reagan
8 Sylvester Stallone
9 Andrew Lloyd Webber
10 Torvill and Dean
11 Max Bygraves

All Futura Books are available at your bookshop or newsagent, or can be ordered from the following address:
Futura Books, Cash Sales Department,
P.O. Box 11, Falmouth, Cornwall.

Please send cheque or postal order (no currency), and allow 45p for postage and packing for the first book plus 20p for the second book and 14p for each additional book ordered up to a maximum charge of £1.63 in U.K.

Customers in Eire and B.F.P.O. please allow 45p for the first book, 20p for the second book plus 14p per copy for the next 7 books, thereafter 8p per book.

Overseas customers please allow 75p for postage and packing for the first book and 21p per copy for each additional book.